IMAGES
of America

ROUTE 66
IN MISSOURI

ON THE COVER: These bathing beauties pose at the Stonydell Pool near Arlington. On the right is Lois Crick Gore, formerly of Richland, Missouri. The other is unidentified. George Prewett built the amazing stonework and the 100-foot-long pool in 1932. It was demolished for the construction of Interstate 44 in 1967, but the icy cold spring that fed it still burbles up through a pipe on the south side of Old 66. (Author's collection.)

IMAGES
of America

ROUTE 66
IN MISSOURI

Joe Sonderman

ARCADIA
PUBLISHING

Published by Arcadia Publishing
Charleston, South Carolina

Printed in the United States of America

Library of Congress Control Number: 2018958884

For all general information, please contact Arcadia Publishing:
Telephone 843-853-2070
Fax 843-853-0044
E-mail sales@arcadiapublishing.com
For customer service and orders:
Toll-Free 1-888-313-2665

Visit us on the Internet at www.arcadiapublishing.com

In memory of Gary Turner, Bob Waldmire, and Lillian Redman.

CONTENTS

ACKNOWLEDGMENTS

Special thanks to Cheryl Eichar Jett for her constant encouragement and the idea! Special thanks to Renee McHenry at the Missouri Department of Transportation, Sharon Smith at the Missouri Historical Society in St. Louis, and the staff at the Missouri State Archives. Thanks to Mike Ward and Steve Rider for their generosity in sharing images. Also, thanks to "roadies" Jim Ross, Jerry McClanahan, Rich Dinkela, Shellee Graham, Sharon Ward, Russell Olsen, Nick Gerlich, Jim Conkle, and David Wickline. Thanks as well to Jim Kempert at Arcadia Publishing.

Unless otherwise noted, all images are from the author's collection.

INTRODUCTION

Missouri is the birthplace of Route 66, and the "Show Me State" has plenty to show the Route 66 traveler. The historic highway runs from the Mississippi River and the big city of St. Louis across the forested hills and crystal clear streams of the Ozarks.

The Osage first blazed a trail atop a ridge that ran between the Ozarks and the confluence of the Missouri and Mississippi Rivers. Cherokee forced to move from the Southeastern United States to Indian Territory in present-day Oklahoma made the bitter journey on the "Trail of Tears" along part of this route in the 1830s. In 1837, the state authorized a road between St. Louis and Springfield following the Kickapoo Trail or Osage Trail.

When the telegraph arrived, the stage route between St. Louis and Springfield became known as the Wire Road. The Blue and the Gray marched along its dusty path to battle at Carthage, Wilson's Creek, and in countless skirmishes. Bushwhackers terrorized the land. By the 1880s, resorts were springing up along the Gasconade and Big Piney Rivers serviced by the St. Louis & San Francisco Railroad. They were popular destinations for sportsmen from the big cities, but the Ozarks were still inaccessible to the masses.

The first automobiles came to Missouri in 1891, and there were over 16,000 registered by 1911. Clem H. Laessig opened the first gas station in the United States at 412 Theresa Street in St. Louis in 1905. In 1919, the American Automobile Association (AAA) opened a tourist camp in St. Louis's Forest Park. Early motorists derided as "tin can tourists" often just camped beside the road where they pleased. Farmers began building cabins, often adding gas pumps and a café.

Meanwhile, confusion reigned. Promoters laid out highways of their own, charging merchants or towns to be on the route and often taking motorists miles out of their way. They gave their roads colorful names and splashed logos on fence posts, telegraph poles, or any other handy surface. Often, very little was spent on maintenance.

In 1917, the Ozark Trail Association mapped out a system of routes between St. Louis and Romeroville, New Mexico. From there, the Ozark Trail Route joined the National Old Trails Road to Los Angeles. By 1918, a segment of the Ozark Trail was paved from Webb City through Joplin to the Kansas state line.

In 1920, Missouri voters approved a measure creating a state highway system to "Lift Missouri Out of the Mud." In 1922, the state highway commission designated routes connecting the big cities. The road between St. Louis and Joplin became State Route 14.

The federal government stepped in to bring order to the map in 1925. Meeting in St. Louis, the American Association of State Highway Officials approved a numbering system for the proposed federal highways.

A dispute arose over the number for the route from Chicago to Los Angeles proposed by influential highway official Cyrus Avery of Oklahoma. It was settled when Missouri and Oklahoma officials met in Springfield on April 30, 1926, and noticed that the catchy sounding "66" was still available. Springfield thus became the "Birthplace of Route 66."

Route 66 was far from the "Main Street of America" envisioned by Cyrus Avery at the time. There were just 64 miles of pavement on Route 66 between California and the Texas line. In Missouri, only about two thirds of the route was paved.

Marketing made Route 66 a legend. John T. Woodruff, Springfield civic leader and owner of the Kentwood Arms Hotel, became the first president of the US 66 Highway Association. The organization coined the phrase "The Main Street of America."

The association became involved in a transcontinental footrace promoted by C.C. "Cash and Carry" Pyle. The grueling 3,422-mile race from Los Angeles to New York, including all of Route 66, established the highway in the pop culture pantheon. The part-Cherokee Andy Payne from Foyil, Oklahoma, won the race. Pyle went broke.

Missouri was the third state to completely pave 66 within its borders. The final section was completed on January 5, 1931, in Phelps County near Arlington. More than 7,000 people attended a celebration in Rolla on March 15 to mark the occasion.

John Steinbeck's book and the subsequent film *The Grapes of Wrath* forever linked Route 66 with images of overloaded jalopies and struggling Dust Bowl refugees. But it provided opportunity for some in Missouri, from roadside entrepreneurs to job seekers headed for the massive dam construction at Bagnell on the Osage River.

World War II brought much more traffic and deadly accidents. The first four-lane divided section was constructed to speed traffic serving Fort Leonard Wood in 1943. It included the largest highway cut on a US highway at the time, blasting through the solid rock near Hooker.

Many of those soldiers who served at Fort Leonard Wood would return with their families to vacation in the Ozarks after World War II. These were the glory years of Route 66. Roadside hucksterism was at its height. Travelers were demanding more than just a ramshackle cabin, and the motels and attractions pulled out all the stops to stand out. The roadside blazed with neon.

Bobby Troup gave Route 66 its greatest publicity boost. The jazz musician and aspiring songwriter was headed to Los Angeles to try and make his mark when his wife, Cynthia, suggested he write a song about Route 40. Troup said they would soon be traveling on Route 66 and Cynthia came up with "Get Your Kicks on Route 66." Originally a hit for Nat King Cole in 1946, the song has been recorded by dozens of other artists, including St. Louis rock and roll legend Chuck Berry.

But not everyone was welcome. African Americans faced inconvenient, embarrassing, and sometimes life-threatening conditions. Most avoided the "sundown" towns that used laws and intimidation to keep blacks out. *The Negro Motorist Green Book* listed businesses willing to serve black travelers, but there were few in rural Missouri.

Route 66 became a victim of its own success. It gained the nickname "Bloody 66" as the toll from crashes increased. On August 2, 1956, Missouri became the first state to award a contract under the Interstate Highway Act for work on four-lane Route 66 in Laclede County. The nation's first actual interstate highway construction took place west of the Missouri River on I-70 at St. Charles.

Missouri was not giving up on 66 just yet. In December 1962, the state petitioned federal officials to designate the route as Interstate 66. The feds refused. The towns along Route 66 between Carthage and Springfield threatened to sue to keep the US 66 designation, and highway officials responded by building I-44 farther south. By 1965, those towns were completely bypassed.

By 1972, Interstate 44 had replaced 66 across Missouri. In June 1974, the American Association of State Highway and Transportation Officials (AASHTO) eliminated US Route 66 from Chicago to Joplin. Few noticed when the Route 66 signs on the short remaining segment came down in July 1985.

Interstate 44 replaced Old 66 in Missouri, but it could not kill it. Drivers continued to go out of their way to connect with the people and travel through the heart of the towns. By 1990, there was enough interest to form the Route 66 Association of Missouri "To preserve, promote and develop old Route 66 in Missouri." Today, the association and Route 66 "roadies" are dedicated to preserving the road for future generations.

One

ST. LOUIS

1933–1955 SOUTHERN OR HISTORIC ROUTE

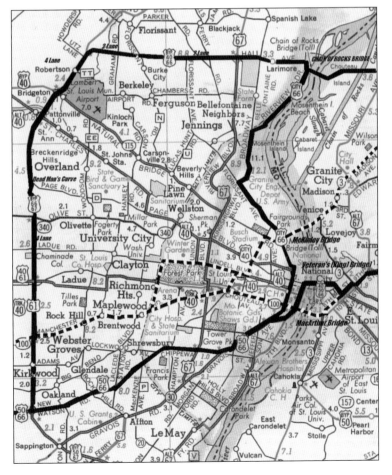

Alignments through St. Louis are plentiful and difficult to sort out. This map shows the highway system in 1955. The three alignments current at the time are outlined in heavy black lines. Lindbergh Boulevard had become Bypass 66, City 66 came in from North St. Louis, and the mainline headed west on Watson Road. Broken lines represent earlier alignments and the 1926 route using Manchester Road west.

Route 66 originally used the McKinley Bridge. In 1929, the route shifted to the Municipal Bridge, renamed the MacArthur Bridge in 1942. A small diner at Seventh Street and Chouteau Avenue at first mainly served railroad workers. It has not changed much since becoming the Eat Rite in 1940 with the motto "Eat Rite or Don't Eat at All." The Eat Rite closed in October 2017 but reopened under new ownership in April 2018.

Purina Mills founder William Danforth used a checkerboard to symbolize his belief in balancing people's physical, social, mental, and religious lives. His feed company became Ralston-Purina in 1902, when he started making cereal with Webster Edgerly, founder of the Ralstonism health movement. The headquarters of Ralston-Purina became famous as Checkerboard Square and are seen here looking west from the MacArthur Bridge. The firm merged with Nestle in December 2001.

The first drive-in "filling station" in the world opened in 1905 on South Theresa Avenue at Market Street in St. Louis. Clemons Harry Laessig came up with the idea of using gravity-fed tanks and a simple garden hose at the American Automotive Gasoline Company he founded with partner Harry C. Grenner. At the time, there were about 300 automobiles in St. Louis. Shell Oil Company purchased the firm in 1929 and the station was demolished by 1949. (Shell Oil Company.)

On August 24, 1951, the opening of the Southtown Famous-Barr store at Kingshighway Boulevard and Chippewa Street (City 66) brought out 15,000 shoppers. The streamlined three-story building closed on January 18, 1992, and was demolished in 1995 for a proposed big-box store that was never built. The site remained vacant until the Southtown Centre strip mall opened in 2004. (Museum of Transportation.)

Hampton Village was the first shopping center in St. Louis. It began as a farmers market developed by Harold Brinkop in 1939 at Hampton Avenue and Chippewa Street. Bettendorf's opened a supermarket there in 1940. From 1946 to 1962, similar Colonial-style buildings also stood on the southwest corner where Target is today. The southeast portion, shown here, still looks much the same. (Missouri Historical Society.)

Walt Anderson and Billy Ingram founded White Castle in Wichita, Kansas, in 1921. White symbolized purity at a time when hamburger restaurants had an unsavory reputation. White Castle No. 24, at Hampton Village, was the best known of the St. Louis Route 66 locations. It opened on November 13, 1937. This location offered car hops and curb service until 1970 and was torn down in November 1983. (White Castle Archives.)

St. Louis Cardinals great Stan Musial was a frequent guest at Biggie's 66 Café at 6435 Chippewa Street, operated by his friend Julius "Biggie" Garagnani. In January 1949, they became partners, and the café became Stan Musial and Biggies Restaurant. They later moved to 5130 Oakland Avenue. The Chippewa Street site shown here became a Flaming Pit Restaurant, and a medical building is located on the site today. (Missouri Historical Society.)

When the old common fields of St. Louis were subdivided, the east-west streets that were created were named after Indian tribes. The Donut Drive-In at 6526 Chippewa Street opened in 1952. With help from a National Park Service Route 66 corridor preservation grant, the sign with its animated red neon donuts was restored in 2008. Another federal grant helped restore the facade in 2016. (John, Paul, Jim, and Chuck Schwarz.)

Local amateur tennis champ Ted Drewes Sr. opened his first frozen custard stand on Natural Bridge Avenue in 1930, followed by a location on South Grand Avenue in 1931. The Watson Road location shown here opened in 1941 and is the best known Route 66 landmark in St. Louis. In 1959, Ted Drewes Jr. invented the concrete, a shake so thick it can be turned upside down. In TV ads, Ted Jr. said, "It really is good guys—and gals!"

In 1934, Gus Belt opened the first Steak 'n Shake in Normal, Illinois. The meat was ground in front of the customers; the slogan was "In Sight It Must Be Right." The first St. Louis location opened on December 4, 1948, at Chippewa Street and Landsdowne Avenue. A second store opened in 1949 at Chippewa Street and Morganford Road. The first St. Louis location burned in 2002, and the site is now a Starbucks. (Missouri Historical Society.)

The first paving project by the State of Missouri within the St. Louis city limits began on August 31, 1932. It took a Missouri Supreme Court ruling before state money could be used for projects in big cities. The work had to be a continuation of a state route and in a sparsely populated area. As seen in this view looking east across the River des Peres, the new Watson Road and southwest St. Louis met the criteria at that time. (Missouri State Archives.)

The St. Louis & San Francisco Railroad (the "Frisco") built this timber trestle over the new Watson Road in 1931, and it is still in use today. The Frisco Railroad is synonymous with Route 66 in Missouri, as the highway often parallels the tracks. The Burlington Northern Railroad took over the Frisco in 1980. In 2017, the City of Shrewsbury constructed an overlook here for train watchers on Route 66. (Missouri State Archives.)

The Coral Court was one of the finest motels on Route 66. Opened by John Carr in 1942, each unit could be entered directly from a private garage. Along with its short-term rates, that feature gave the Coral Court a beloved but racy reputation late in its life. The Coral Court closed on August 20, 1993, and was demolished for a subdivision. One partly reconstructed unit is displayed at the Museum of Transportation in St. Louis County. (Steve Rider Collection.)

In September 1953, Carl Austin Hall and Bonnie Heady kidnapped and killed six-year-old Bobby Greenlease, son of a wealthy Kansas City car dealer. Hall holed up at the Coral Court with a prostitute the night before their arrest and insisted he had most of the $600,000 ransom when he was captured, but half of the money had disappeared. Hall and Heady went to the gas chamber, and the missing money was never found.

Between 1939 and 1941, seven motels were constructed on a three-mile strip of Watson Road through Marlborough. The Duplex Motel, the Wayside Court, the Chippewa Motel, and La Casa Grande still stand. The 66 Auto Court, at 8730 Watson Road, closed in 1978, and firefighters burned it down for a training exercise in 1981. The site is now the Watson Auto Care Plaza, and a replica of the sign stands on the Old Chain of Rocks Bridge.

Rock and roll history was made in a little cinder block building next to the 66 Park-In at lower right. Radio station KSHE originally broadcast classical music aimed at females, hence the "SHE." In 1967, it became one of the first underground rock stations. KSHE helped break acts such as REO Speedwagon and Sammy Hagar. The studio window was a hangout for youths until operations moved to Union Station in 1986.

On September 26, 1947, the Flexer Drive In Corporation opened the 66 Park-In at 9438 Watson Road. The first film shown was *Lady Luck*, starring Robert Young. Designed by St. Louis architect William Mills, the 18-acre 66 Park-In offered a tiny train, a Ferris wheel, and a trained bear cub. A few months later, Flexer sold to Fred Wehrenberg. The screen was demolished for a retail development on March 19, 1994.

Crestwood Plaza opened in 1957 on a site once partly occupied by Emil Richter's 66 Worm Ranch. The center doubled in size in 1967 and was enclosed in 1984. The complex then included 140 stores and a five-screen theater. The mall faced increased competition, and needed improvements were never made. In April 2012, Sears became the last anchor store to close, and the mall was demolished in 2016. As of 2018, the site remained vacant.

Pro bowlers Dick Weber, Pat Patterson, and Rich Volling opened Crestwood Bowl in 1958. Weber and Patterson were on the St. Louis Budweisers team that rolled a 3858 team series in 1958, a record that stood for 38 years. Ray Bluth, also a member of the Budweisers, took over in 1973. His son Mike still runs the lanes. The Route 66 Association of Missouri and the National Park Service helped restore the sign in 2012.

Missouri's first McDonald's and the 71st in the nation opened on August 30, 1958, at 9915 Watson Road. Don R. Kuehl and Bill Wyatt's location, like all the early stores, was a walk-up only, with an all-male staff. Franchise founder Ray Kroc believed female employees would attract boys and turn the stores into teen hangouts. The building was replaced in 1978, but this is still a busy McDonald's location today.

Ralph Stille opened the first Chuck-a-Burger Drive-In at Page and Pennsylvania Avenues in 1955. The third location, at 9955 Watson Road (pictured), opened in 1958. There eventually were eight Chuck-a-Burger locations, but only the store at 9025 St. Charles Rock Road survives today, operated by Ralph's son Ron Stille. The Crestwood location became a Kentucky Fried Chicken and then O'Reilly Auto Parts.

The Park Plaza Courts at Lindbergh Boulevard and Watson Road opened in 1948 and were part of a chain modeled on the Alamo and spaced a day's drive apart, mostly on Route 66. It became the Ozark Plaza Motel in 1963 and was demolished in 1971 for the Holiday Inn–Viking, today's Holiday Inn Southwest–Route 66. Nelson's Café next door became the Flame in 1960 and then the Viking Restaurant. The Twisted Tree Steakhouse is located here today.

On August 20, 1931, the first cloverleaf interchange west of the Mississippi opened at Watson Road and Lindbergh Boulevard (Missouri 77). A sign on northbound Lindbergh Boulevard read, "To Go West (Left) Go Thru Intersection and Make Two Right Turns." In 1936, it became the junction of US 66 (Lindbergh Boulevard) and City Route 66 (Watson Road). The attractive overpass trimmed with pink granite was replaced in 1980. (Missouri State Archives.)

In 1963, crews are grading and removing some of the 1.9 million cubic yards of solid rock blasted away for the interchange of Interstate 44/US 66 and Interstate 244, now I-270. The interchange was completed in the summer of 1964, but it would be 1971 before Interstate 44 linked to downtown St. Louis. I-270 was completed in 1968, and the I-44/I-270 interchange was rebuilt in 1998. (Missouri State Archives.)

Sylvan Beach Park on the Meramec River offered a miniature steam train, speedboat rides, and even dirt track midget auto races. It closed in 1954 when the new bridge creating four-lane Highway 66 was built. The restaurant remained until 1962. The pool became the Fontainebleau Swim Club and then the Kirkwood Municipal Pool, even though it was in Sunset Hills. The Sylvan Beach site is now Emmenegger Nature Park. (Richard Zimmer.)

St. Louis County police officers pose with their new 1962 Plymouth Fury patrol cars at the Chrysler assembly plant in Fenton. It opened on July 1, 1959. The truck assembly plant, or North Plant, opened in 1966. The two facilities once employed over 6,000 people on a 341-acre site. Production at the South Assembly Plant ended in October 2008. The North Plant closed in July 2009, and the complex was demolished. (Missouri State Archives.)

George Madden lost his St. Louis saloon license for staying open late in 1937, then opened Dudley's at Route 66 and Bowles Avenue. On June 25, 1941, race track tout Charles "Cutie" Bailey was found shot to death on the highway nearby after he left Dudley's with gangsters Thomas Whalen and Patrick Hogan. George Madden was a witness for the state at Hogan's trial. Madden accidently drowned in the Meramec River in 1943.

Antire Hill, shown here, is part of 24 miles of connected recreation areas known as the Henry Shaw Ozark Corridor. It includes Lone Elk Park, the World Bird Sanctuary, the Endangered Wolf Center, West Tyson County Park, and the Forest 44 Conservation Area. Washington University's Tyson Research Center is used for ecological studies on a site where ammunition was stored during World War II. (Missouri State Archives.)

The Bridgehead Inn at the Meramec River opened in 1936 and was originally known for gambling and other vices. Earl Tedrow, former owner of Beecher's Log Cabin Inn at Valley Park, bought it in 1941. Edward "Steiny" Steinberg moved in after his restaurant across the river burned in 1947. Later the Galley West Restaurant, the old roadhouse was headquarters for the dioxin cleanup in Times Beach and is now the Route 66 State Park visitor's center.

The Warren deck truss bridge at Times Beach in the background was completed in 1932. A bridge for eastbound traffic was under construction at the time of this 1956 photograph. After I-44 was finished, the old span served the town of Times Beach and then Route 66 State Park. But it was allowed to deteriorate and closed in 2009 for safety reasons. The deck was removed in 2013 to buy time for preservation efforts.

Times Beach began as a promotion by the old *St. Louis Times* newspaper offering a 20-by-100-foot lot for $67.50 with a six-month subscription. In 1971, Russell Bliss was hired to spread waste oil on the dusty streets. After a flood in 1982, residents learned the oil was contaminated with dioxin. The government leveled the community of about 2,200. After a $110-million cleanup, the site became Route 66 State Park.

Deke Keeton built the Rock City Café, cabins, and gas station between the Frisco and Missouri Pacific tracks east of Eureka. Ed LaMar's Ozark Café and tourist court, tavern, and gas station were immediately to the east. The buildings were similar, so both businesses became known as Rock City. It was demolished for construction of the four-lane highway in 1955. The women in this photograph are unidentified.

Eureka High School overlooks the new four-lane Route 66. Part of the Log Cabin Cafe is at far right. It was owned by major leaguer Bob Klinger during the 1940s and leased by the Gerwes and Hanephin families. Klinger was pitching for Boston in game seven of the 1946 World Series when Enos Slaughter made his mad dash from first to score the winning run on a hit by Harry Walker. Klinger died in an auto accident on Missouri 100 at Villa Ridge in 1977.

Super Sports Cars on Route 66 were part of the fun when the Six Flags over Mid-America amusement park opened on June 5, 1971. Six Flags spurred a major building boom in Eureka, but it doomed traditional amusement parks such as Chain of Rocks Fun Fair in St. Louis. Now Six Flags St. Louis, the park bills itself as the coaster capital of Missouri, with nine roller coasters. It also boasts a massive water park.

In September 1934, former bootleggers James and William Smith opened the Red Cedar Tavern at the east end of Pacific, built with red cedar logs. James Smith Jr. took over and hired Katherine Brinkman as a waitress. They married in 1940, and the business remained in the family until closing on March 7, 2005. The City of Pacific purchased the structure in 2017 and was planning to open a local history and Route 66 museum.

The Beacon Court is mostly a memory, but its sign lives on. It opened in 1946 with 16 units and a sign made from an old windmill derrick topped with a beacon. George and Monica Mahler saved the 27-foot-tall sign after the motel closed, and it now stands at the Beacon Car and Pet Wash at 675 East Osage Street. Only a portion of the old motel office and the driveway remain today. (Library of Congress, John Margolies Collection.)

Pacific was originally known as Franklin, and the name was changed when the Pacific Railroad arrived in 1859. The photograph above looks west on Osage Street from First Street prior to construction of the new Route 66. By August 6, 1933, traffic was using the new alignment shown below, and a gala celebration took place on August 12. The celebration at the foot of Sand Mountain included a "5 Negro Battle Royal" and a street dance.

State commercial vehicle enforcement officers pose in front of the sandstone bluffs of the Meramec River along Route 66 at Pacific. Since the 1870s, the bluffs have been mined for silica sand used in fine glassware. Caves created by mining were exposed when Route 66 cut through the bluff. Some are used for storage today, because the temperature inside remains constant at about 60 degrees. (Missouri State Archives.)

Route 66 was lined with flowers and trees between the Missouri Botanical Garden in St. Louis and the garden's arboretum at Gray Summit (now Shaw Nature Preserve). It was called the Henry Shaw Gardenway in honor of the garden founder. In 1939, an overlook at Pacific was named in honor of Lars Peter Jensen, who ran the arboretum and the Gardenway Association. The overlook was closed for 25 years but reopened in 2016.

Two

ST. LOUIS
1936–1955 MAINLINE AND
1955–1965 BYPASS ROUTES

"The Chain of Rocks Bridge," Highway 66 over Mississippi River near St. Louis, Mo.   BL 76

There are many stories about the 24-degree bend in the middle of the Chain of Rocks Bridge. It was actually ordered by the government so the bridge faced the main channel where the Mississippi River washes over a hazardous rock ledge. The bridge opened on July 20, 1929, and carried Route 66 from 1936 to 1955. This route was Bypass 66 from 1955 to 1965. A canal allowing river traffic to bypass the rocks opened in 1953.

For the town of Madison, Illinois, toll revenue made the Chain of Rocks a golden goose. This view shows traffic after the tolls were lifted but before the Interstate 270 bridge opened on September 2, 1966. Only a drop in scrap metal prices kept the historic span from being demolished. Gateway Trailnet leased it in 1997, and the 5,353-foot-long Old Chain of Rocks is now one of the world's longest pedestrian and bicycle bridges.

Chain of Rocks Amusement Park, later Chain of Rocks Fun Fair, was on top of the bluff overlooking the bridge. During the 1960s and 1970s, the park was a popular place for school and church picnics. Doomed by Six Flags over Mid-America, a couple of fires, and burdensome St. Louis city taxes, Chain of Rocks Fun Fair closed on Labor Day 1977. A housing development occupies the site today.

Two towers in the Mississippi River below the Chain of Rocks Bridge were once intakes for the St. Louis Water Works. William Eames designed Tower One, which looks like a castle and was erected in 1896. In the background, Tower Two resembles a Roman villa and was erected in 1915. The river is much higher today due to a low-water dam that keeps the Chain of Rocks Canal at sufficient depth.

The route across north St. Louis County followed present-day Dunn Road and turned south on Lindbergh Boulevard. The north section of the route included a cloverleaf interchange with Superhighway 99 to St. Louis or to Alton, Illinois. At the time of this 1956 photograph, it was the interchange of US 67 and Bypass 66. Today, this view would be looking south at Missouri 367 and Interstate 270. (Missouri State Archives.)

The new Missouri 77/Lindbergh Boulevard cut through farmland in 1934. This view looks north from the Wabash (Norfolk & Southern) underpass in Robertson. This area, where McDonnell Aircraft would construct its distinctive headquarters in 1955, is now part of Hazelwood. Joseph Burcke ran the general store at right. The barn is at the intersection with Brown Road, now McDonnell Boulevard. (Missouri State Archives.)

Maj. Albert Bond Lambert leased a site in 1920 and developed the St. Louis Flying Field at his own expense. He bought the property in 1925 and later sold it to the City of St. Louis at cost. The Lambert Field terminal on Bridgeton Station Road opened in 1933 and could handle four planes at once. It was replaced by the new terminal on the south side of the airport in 1956 and was demolished in 1979. The plane is a Curtiss Condor.

James S. McDonnell Jr. started his aircraft company in 1939 with one employee and no contracts. By 1964, McDonnell Aircraft employed over 40,000 workers. They built the Mercury and Gemini space capsules and military jets like the F2H Banshee, F-101 Voodoo, and F-4 Phantom II. McDonnell merged with Douglas Aircraft in 1967, and Boeing took over in late 1996. Boeing employs about 14,000 people locally today. (McDonnell-Douglas Photograph.)

Some of the Apollo astronauts stayed at the Stanley Cour-Tel while visiting McDonnell Aircraft. Stanley and Olivia Williams ran the motel at Lindbergh Boulevard and Natural Bridge Road from 1950 until 1976. It was demolished in 2002, along with 2,000 homes and dozens of businesses, for the controversial expansion of the St. Louis Lambert International Airport. Lindbergh Boulevard was relocated to run through a tunnel under the runway.

Edna Bulan operated a restaurant across from Lambert Field named after the *Winnie Mae*, the plane flown by her friend, famed aviator Wiley Post. She also provided food service at the airfield. The restaurant is the building with the gables facing the airport and Bridgeton Station Road. The brick building behind it facing Lindbergh Boulevard was part of Bulan's Motel from 1949 until the airport expanded in 1968.

Lindbergh Boulevard crosses over Interstate 70 a few miles east of the birthplace of the interstate system that doomed Route 66. The first actual construction under the Interstate Highway Act began on Interstate 70 west of the Missouri River at St. Charles, Missouri, on August 13, 1956. This view looks west on I-70 at Lindbergh (By-Pass 66) in 1960. (Missouri State Archives.)

Northwest Plaza, at Lindbergh Boulevard and St. Charles Rock Road, was the largest shopping center in the world when it opened in 1965. Enclosed in 1989, it faded in the 2000s amid changing demographics, online shopping, and big-box stores. The last store closed in November 2010. The distinctive dome of the former Famous-Barr store is one of the remaining structures now part of the Crossings at Northwest development.

Lindbergh Boulevard/Missouri 77 plunged downhill and curved sharply under the railroad in Ascalon, now part of Maryland Heights. After this section became US 66 and was widened to four lanes, it became notorious as the "Dead Man's Stretch." A new roadway with guardrails and an interchange at Page Avenue was completed in April 1963. Completion of Interstate 244 in 1968 also eased traffic through the once-deadly section. (Missouri State Archives.)

The Smith Brothers Motel was at the intersection of four major US routes, 40-61 and 66-67, and opened in 1943. Lester Neiman and Alvin Block bought the property in 1945 and named it the King Brothers Motel. It grew to a complex that could accommodate over 600 guests. In 1974, developer Donald Breckenridge incorporated parts of it into his Breckenridge Inn, now the Hilton St. Louis–Frontenac.

In 1933, traffic was light enough that a caramel corn vendor could sell his wares at Lindbergh Boulevard and Manchester Road. Manchester Road had just lost its US 66 designation to the new Watson Road but kept the US 50 shields. Lindbergh Boulevard was carrying US 61 and Missouri 77 and would become US 66 three years later. The billboard promotes Missouri 99, now Missouri 367, as the best route to Alton, Illinois. (Missouri State Archives.)

After Route 66 was shifted from Manchester to Watson Road, merchants on the original alignment fought unsuccessfully to have Manchester designated as US 66 North. This photograph was taken in 1933 looking west on Manchester Road at Lindbergh Boulevard. The Wedge restaurant occupied a triangle-shaped parcel formed by a dedicated turn lane from northbound Lindbergh Boulevard to eastbound Manchester Road. The triangle forming the wedge still exists today. (Missouri State Archives.)

Louie McGinley invented the curb service tray, and in 1930, opened the area's first drive-in restaurant, the Parkmoor at Clayton Road and Big Bend Boulevard. Eventually there were six locations, including two on Route 66. Those were at Chippewa Street and Plainview Avenue and at Lindbergh Boulevard and Manchester Road, shown here. The original location was the last survivor and was demolished in 1999. (The Parkmoor.)

Because Kirkwood did not agree to change the name of the road to Lindbergh, the route becomes Kirkwood Road within the city. Two-lane Route 66 crossing the Frisco and Missouri Pacific Railroad lines at grade was a major bottleneck. The first planned suburb west of the Mississippi was named for James Pugh Kirkwood, the chief engineer of the Pacific Railroad. Also in Kirkwood, Spencer's Grill has been a landmark since 1947. (Missouri Historical Society.)

Looking north on Lindbergh Boulevard (By-Pass 66) from Watson Road (US 66) in 1956, the Park Plaza Motel and Nelson's Café are at left. On the right is the sign for the Westward Motel, opened in 1953. The motel was demolished in 1998, and a Hampton Inn stands there today. The restored sign can be seen at the National Museum of Transportation on Barrett Station Road, near the original alignment of Route 66. (Missouri State Archives.)

40

Three

ST. LOUIS
1926–1933 ORIGINAL ROUTE

Original Route 66 and a later optional route used the McKinley Bridge and followed Salisbury Street to Natural Bridge Boulevard. Crown Candy Kitchen is just off Original 66 at Fourteenth Street and St. Louis Avenue. Harry Karandzieff and his friend Pete Jugaloff opened the confectionery and restaurant here in 1913, and it is still in the Karandzieff family. Anyone who can drink five 24-ounce malts or shakes in 30 minutes gets them free.

Early Route 66 turned from Natural Bridge Road to Grand Boulevard opposite Fairgrounds Park. The St. Louis Agricultural and Mechanical Association presented big annual exhibitions in the park from 1856 to 1902 except during the Civil War. The city's first zoo was located here. A race riot at the newly integrated Fairgrounds Park Pool in June 1949 was a turning point in local civil rights history. (Missouri Historical Society.)

Baseball has been played at Grand Boulevard and Dodier Street since the 1860s. The American League Browns and the National League Cardinals shared Sportsman's Park from 1920 until 1953, when the Browns left for Baltimore and it became the first Busch Stadium. The Cardinals played their last game here on May 8, 1966. It was also the home of the football Cardinals from 1960 until 1965. The site is now the Herbert Hoover Boys and Girls Club. (Stupp Brothers Archives.)

The Fox Theater is located a couple of blocks from where the early alignments of Route 66 turned west onto Delmar Boulevard. The 5,000 seat "Fabulous Fox" was reported to be the second largest theater in the United States when it opened on January 31, 1929. It closed in 1978 but was restored by new owners Leon and Mary Strauss and Harvey Davis. It reopened in September 1982 and in 1986 hosted an all-star tribute concert to Chuck Berry featured in the film *Hail, Hail Rock and Roll*. (Missouri Historical Society.)

In September 1915, the largest electric sign west of the Mississippi at the time was erected on Lindell Boulevard immediately east of Grand Boulevard. The 103-foot-long sign with letters six feet tall advertised Ajax tires "Guaranteed for 5000 Miles" at the Guenther-Methudy Sales Company at 3553 Lindell Boulevard. The site is now part of the St. Louis University Dog Park and Sculpture Garden. (Missouri Historical Society.)

The former mansion in the background at 4228 Lindell Boulevard housed the Automobile Club of Missouri from 1938 until it burned in 1975. Its Modernist replacement is still a landmark. AAA posted the signs in the early days of the system, so each of the federal routes was marked to pass by their headquarters. (Missouri Historical Society.)

The first stoplight in St. Louis is visible here at lower left. It went into service in October 1922. Work began on the new cathedral at Lindell Boulevard and Newstead Avenue on May 1, 1907, and it was consecrated on June 29, 1926. Pope John Paul II designated it the Cathedral Basilica of St. Louis in 1997 and visited during his historic trip in October 1999. (Library of Congress.)

The Chase–Park Plaza Hotel at Lindell and Kingshighway Boulevards was the glamorous center of St. Louis night life. Chase Ullman opened his hotel in 1922. Wealthy guests forced Prohibition agents to retreat in a melee during a raid after midnight on January 1, 1923. Sam Koplar began work on the Park Plaza next door in 1929 and took over the Chase in 1946. They were combined in 1961. Both are restored and operate as one complex today.

An early alignment of Route 66 ran along the north edge of Forest Park, where grand mansions still line Lindell Boulevard. The route then turned south on Skinker Avenue. Forest Park is 450 acres larger than Central Park in New York and hosted 20 million visitors during the 1904 World's Fair. The St. Louis Zoo and the St. Louis Art Museum, both in Forest Park, are among the finest in the world, and admission is free.

The sign on the lubrication building at the Hi-Pointe Standard was 70 feet tall with 5,800 lamps and 2,900 feet of neon tubing. This beacon atop one of the highest points in St. Louis came down when a modern station was constructed in 1959. It was replaced with an equally huge Plexiglas sign that was changed to read "Amoco" in 1985. Operated by Leclaire C. Stephenson from 1951 until 1984, the station is now branded as BP. But the Amoco sign remains a much loved landmark.

Built in 1922, the Hi-Pointe Theatre at 1005 McCausland Avenue is the oldest continuously operating single-screen movie theater in the area. George and Georgia James have owned the theater since 1977. Their daughter Diana and her husband, Bill Grayson, added another screen on the second floor of a building behind the main theater. That part is known as the Hi-Pointe Backlot. (Missouri Historical Society.)

Original 66 turned west onto Manchester Road into Maplewood. When James Sutton died in 1877, he left his land to be divided among his nine children. One of his daughters, Mary C. Marshall, sold her portion to developers, who planted maple trees in a new subdivision. Maplewood was incorporated in 1908. This photograph was taken at Manchester Road and Southwest Avenue in 1929, when Goodyear was promoting its Airwheel, first used on aircraft. (Elmer Wind Jr.)

Katz drugstores were known for catchy advertising slogans and low prices. St. Louis Highway 66 locations included Webster Groves, Kirkwood, and this store on Manchester Road in Maplewood. Operator Ira Stuart is shown on the last night of operations for the Manchester streetcar line in 1949. Katz was sold to Skaggs in 1970. This building is now a restaurant and furniture store. (National Museum of Transportation.)

Cunningham's Lubright developed into one of the area's best loved burger joints. In 1951, it became Walter Breeden's Good Food Drive-In. Carl and Patricia Myer took over in 1959. They changed the name to Carl's and later enclosed the restaurant with just 16 seats. Frank Cunetto has operated Carl's since the 1980s, still serving the famous root beer from an original 1951 refrigerated keg. (Frank Cunetto.)

The Mentor Bar, or Nine Mile House, opened in 1890 where Manchester Road crossed a branch of the Missouri Pacific Railroad. Batista "Tony" and Carolina Porta changed it to Porta's Tavern in 1922. They survived Prohibition by adding pool tables, a dance hall, and a dining room. Their sons Angelo and Joe took over after World War II. George and Kris Hansford have operated the Trainwreck Saloon here since July 2, 1982. (George Hansford.)

The first drive-in theater in the St. Louis area was simply known as the Drive-In when it opened on May 24, 1940, at Manchester and Ballas Roads. It became the Manchester Drive-In in 1949. Interstate 244, now Interstate 270, made the site prime real estate when it opened in 1965. The drive-in was torn down in 1967. West County Center, with its landmark sign of a stylized dove, opened here in 1969. (Missouri Historical Society.)

Manchester was originally known as Hoardstown after settler Jesse Hoard. In 1825, it was named after another settler's home town in England. Looking west, the two-story Lyceum Building on the left was built by John Straszer in 1894 and housed businesses on the first floor and a community auditorium on the second. The City of Manchester purchased and restored the landmark in 1977, and it is now city hall.

Original Route 66 runs south of present Missouri 100 through Grover and Pond, now part of Wildwood. The Big Chief Highway Hotel opened in 1928 as the model for the Pierce-Pennant Oil Company chain. It had 62 units with garages renting for $1.50 a night. The motel units were demolished in the 1970s. It was the Big Chief Dakota Grill from 1996 to 2004. Stephanie Mullholland took over in 2012, and it is now the Big Chief Roadhouse.

Tucker Hill east of Villa Ridge presented a major hurdle for road builders. It required a terraced cut 700 feet long, 60 feet deep, and 260 feet wide, the biggest in the United States at the time. A gravel road was ready in July 1927, but paving had to wait for two years to allow the cut through the soft sandstone to settle or cure. Due to road construction over the years, the spot is unrecognizable today. (Missouri State Archives.)

Four

ST. LOUIS

CITY 66 ROUTES

From 1936 until 1963, the northern City Route 66 alignment headed south on Riverview Drive and Broadway before turning onto Calvary Avenue between two historic cemeteries. Those at rest in Bellefontaine Cemetery include William Clark, James B. Eads, and Adolphus Busch. William T. Sherman and Dred Scott are among the notables in Calvary Cemetery. City Route 66 then turned onto West Florissant Avenue. (Missouri Historical Society.)

David G. Nelson's garage at West Florissant and Taylor Avenues, at right, was one of the first locally to provide 24-hour emergency road service. Joseph R. Clooney operated it from 1930 until 1975, and it closed in the 1980s. To avoid heavy traffic, City 66 made a short jog south onto Warne Avenue, turned east onto Carter Avenue and angled back onto West Florissant Avenue, which became North Florissant Avenue.

City 66 swings onto the old Twelfth Street, renamed for former St. Louis mayor Raymond Tucker in 1979. This view looking north on Tucker Boulevard from Carr Street is quite different today. The Illinois Terminal Railroad tunnel beneath the street has been filled in, and Tucker is an attractive landscaped roadway. The Columbus Square Apartments now occupy the area on the right. (Landmarks Association of St. Louis.)

Looking north on Twelfth Street from Market Street, the Jefferson Hotel can be seen at left. In September 1925, a committee meeting at the hotel assigned numbers to the proposed federal routes. The Chicago–Los Angeles route was given US 60, but Kentucky governor William Fields wanted 60 for the route across his state. After a blizzard of telegrams, Missouri and Oklahoma officials agreed to accept 66 on April 30, 1926. (Missouri Historical Society.)

On the left at Twelfth Street (Tucker Boulevard) and Market Street, the Civil Courts Building was completed in 1930. The top is a replica of one of the Seven Wonders of the Ancient World, the tomb of King Mausolus at Halicarnassus in Asia Minor, present-day Turkey. The famous city hall in Los Angeles is also based on the tomb. The courthouse is topped off with a pair of 12-foot-tall griffins with human faces symbolizing human mercy tempering justice.

The Municipal Bridge was the first free crossing of the Mississippi River at St. Louis and opened in 1917. Renamed for Gen. Douglas MacArthur in 1942, it carried alignments of Route 66 from 1929 until 1955. The bridge also carried US 40, 50, and 460. The narrow and tall approaches in Illinois and the sudden jog on the St. Louis side gave it the nickname "Death's Diving Board." (Missouri Historical Society.)

The Veteran's Bridge, shown here under construction, was built by the City of East St. Louis and opened as a toll bridge in 1951. Route 66 was moved to cross this bridge to the Third Street Expressway downtown in 1955. The bridge was renamed in honor of Dr. Martin Luther King Jr. in 1972. To the south, the busy Poplar Street Bridge opened in 1967 and carried Route 66 until 1977. (Stupp Brothers Archives.)

A 37-square-block area along the St. Louis Riverfront was leveled for the Jefferson National Expansion Memorial, now Gateway Arch National Park. Eero Saarinen designed the 630-foot-tall arch covered in stainless steel. The last section was lifted into place on October 28, 1965. A major renovation of the grounds finished in 2018 included a lid over Interstate 44 to reconnect the park and the city. (Missouri State Archives.)

The Cathedral Basilica of St. Louis, popularly known as the "Old Cathedral," was built in 1834. It is the only structure left from when the riverfront was cleared for construction of the Jefferson National Expansion Memorial. This photograph was taken in 1965, shortly after the depressed lanes of Interstate 70 (now Interstate 44) were completed and while the Gateway Arch was still under construction on the right.

Traffic in and out of downtown eased a bit when the 2.3-mile Third Street Expressway opened on October 15, 1955. The first of the postwar expressways to be completed in St. Louis carried Route 66 traffic out of downtown to Gravois Avenue. This view today would be looking westbound just before Interstates 44 and 55 split, with the Gravois exit coming up on the right. The retaining wall at right still stands. (Missouri State Archives.)

Five

Gateway to the Ozarks

Franklin and Crawford Counties

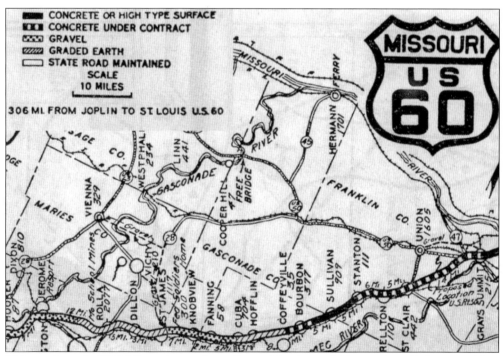

This portion of a 1926 Missouri map shows Route 66 as it was laid out originally between Gray Summit and Arlington. Missouri had already printed up hundreds of maps showing the highway as US 60 prior to a dispute with Kentucky over the route number. Only a small portion of this section at Sullivan had been paved. Long sections of graded earth remained between St. James and Rolla and west of Rolla past Arlington.

Louis Eckelkamp, owner of the famous Diamonds Restaurant, built the first section of the Georgian Revival–style Gardenway Motel near the family home in 1945. The motel, at the west end of the Henry Shaw Gardenway, was expanded in 1953, and large letters on the roof spelling out the name were added when Interstate 44 opened. It closed in 2015 but still stands along with the sign with glass block inserts out front. (Jim Thole.)

Spencer Groff's small "Banana Stand" opened in 1920 at the intersection of two dirt roads and grew into "The World's Largest Roadside Restaurant." The Diamonds Restaurant was named for the shape of the property at Route 66 and Missouri 100 and opened on July 3, 1927. Groff sold to former dishwasher Louis Eckelkamp and Noble Key in 1938. Key later opened the Twin Bridge Café a few miles away. (Washington, Missouri Historical Society.)

Fire destroyed the original Diamonds on February 25, 1948. This new Art Moderne structure formally opened on July 10, 1949. The complex also included a tourist court, the Mission Bell. The Diamonds moved to Interstate 44 in 1967, and Arla and Roscoe Reed moved their Tri County Truck Stop from Sullivan to this site in 1971. The building has been deteriorating since the Tri County closed in 2006.

The Sunset Motel, on present-day Route AT, was built by the Lovelace family and opened in 1945. There are two entrances to each of the 12 units, one opening to the lawn in front and one in the back where the driveway is located. The sign was restored with help from the National Park Service and the Neon Heritage Preservation Committee of the Route 66 Association of Missouri. It was unveiled on November 14, 2009. (Jim Thole.)

HILLTOP SERVICE STATION & GRILL
HIGHWAY 66   37 MILES WEST OF ST. LOUIS   Schuster Studio
Hermann, Mo.

The seven-mile strip of Route 66 between Gray Summit and the Bourbeuse River (pronounced burr-bus) was known as the "Million Dollars a Mile" section based on an estimate of annual sales generated by the roadside businesses. Those included the Villa Courts, the American Inn, Key's Twin Bridges Café, and the Pin Oak Motel. The Hilltop restaurant and service station was one of the businesses that closed within a few weeks after Interstate 44 opened in 1960.

Drivers had to ease off the gas at the twin bridges over the Bourbeuse River. The first seven-panel Pratt through truss span (right) opened in 1925, and its twin (left) was added for eastbound traffic in 1935. A sign on the approach warned "Caution—Careful Driving Required." A new bridge for eastbound traffic opened in 1959 and the old westbound bridge carried the north service road until 1973. US 50 and 66 split west of the bridges. (Missouri State Archives.)

St. Clair was originally known as Traveler's Repose after a wayside inn on the St. Louis–Springfield Road. The name was changed in April 1859 in honor of a resident engineer for the Southwest Branch of the Pacific (Frisco) Railroad. Route 66 was relocated from Main Street to the western edge of town along Commercial Avenue in 1927. The four-lane section shown here west of St. Clair opened in 1952. (Missouri State Archives.)

After 14 years at the International Shoe Company in St. Clair, Virgil Lewis had his fill of shoe leather. In 1938, he partnered with his brother Ralph at the Lewis Place confectionery, which became the Lewis Café. In 1973, Fred and Marie Short (Virgil's nephew and niece-in-law) bought the restaurant. Their son Chris took over in 1996 and started raising the cattle served at the historic eatery.

A tower lit with colorful neon brightens up the North Interstate 44 service road west of St. Clair. Part of the Veterans of Foreign Wars Post 2482 was once the Skylark Motel, opened in 1952 by Robert Johnson after his motel in St. Clair was bypassed. The neon was restored with help from the Neon Heritage Preservation Committee of the Route 66 Association of Missouri and the National Park Service in 2014. (Jim Thole.)

James Scully was a chef at the famous Busch's Grove in St. Louis before he took over Arch Bart's Sunset Inn gas station and restaurant. The original location, shown here, was demolished for construction of the four-lane 66 in 1952, so Scully moved to the new route and added a motel. Scully's closed in 1967, and the place was vacant for 17 years. When it became the Agape House shelter, the old silverware and tablecloths were still in place.

Times were hard in 1932. So when Nazarene minister Paul Jacob Woodcock helped a miner dig up some blue tiff, the miner paid him in rocks. He told Woodcock tourists would snap them up, and so Ozark Rock Curios west of St. Clair was born. Paul was soon shipping specimens around the world, and his wife, Lola May, chipped in by making lamps, clocks, and flowerpots. The business later moved to the four-lane route and then closed in 1977.

OZARK SOUVENIRS AT THE "TEPEE"
55 Miles West of St. Louis, Mo.   Highway No. 66   175 Miles East of Springfield

Schuster Studio
Hermann, Mo.

Clifford Kinney called himself "Injun Joe" and grew a heavy beard to appear more picturesque to the tourists at the Tepee. In October 1941, Clifford's stepson was killed in an auto accident. When Clifford and his wife, Florence, returned from the funeral, she poured kerosene on the stove to start a fire. Both died when it exploded. Clifford's body was found in the cistern, where he dove in trying to extinguish his burning clothes.

There were already three competing caves nearby when Lester Dill leased Salt Peter Cave near Stanton, so some thought he had cave bats in the belfry. With no time to build a parking lot, Lester billed it as Meramec Caverns, the "World's First Drive in Cave." On Memorial Day, 1933, six people paid 40¢ each for a tour. Lester then planted some old rusty relics and declared that outlaw Jesse James had used the cave as a hideout. Dill also is credited with inventing the bumper sticker.

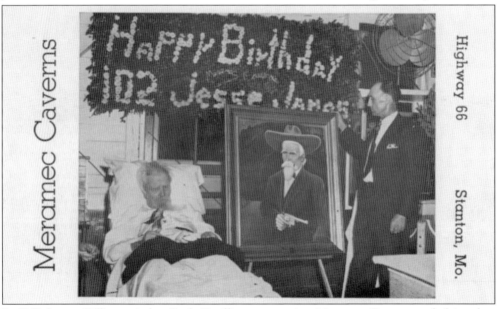

In 1950, Lester Dill's son-in-law Rudy Turilli was operating Meramec Caverns and claimed to have produced Jesse James in person. He brought 102-year-old J. Frank Dalton to a cabin at the cave and asked a judge to legally change Dalton's name to Jesse James. But the judge ruled that if Dalton was the famous badman, his name had never been changed in the first place. Straight-faced guides still tell the Jesse James hideout story at this classic roadside attraction, which is still in the Turilli family.

West of Stanton, Mr. and Mrs. Lewis J. Benson ran Benson's Tourist City, a large complex that included a café that was open around the clock, a gas station, and a trailer camp. They started with four cabins in 1938, and the complex grew to 16 cabins by the time they sold in 1957. It became the McGinnis Sho-Me Courts and was later known as the Del Crest Motel. Some of the buildings still stand.

The White Swan restaurant in Sullivan also served as the local bus stop. It was operated by Fred Snell Sr. and then by his son and became the VFW hall in 1952. Marie Paxton reopened the restaurant and gave it a pink facade with black and white accents in 1956. It was later the White Swan Tavern. The location was a nursery by 1974, and Strauser Drugs, now a Walgreen's, was constructed on the site.

Highway 66 at Sullivan, Missouri

"Awful Good Food" was an odd slogan for a café but it worked for Fred and Jewell Snell. Fred ran a malt shop in Webster Groves before moving to the Rose Restaurant in St. James and then to the White Swan in 1947. The café opened on the new Route 66 in 1949. It was later co-owned by Rudy Turilli and was renamed the Grande Restaurant and then the Hitching Post after the neighboring motel. The building no longer stands.

Marion A. Berti came to America from Medina, Italy, as a young boy and went on to build many stone structures in and around Sullivan. "Grandpa" Berti did beautiful work on the Shamrock Motel, constructed for Freeman Dodds in 1948. John and Rose Weiland took over in 1953, and it was converted to apartments in the late 1970s. As of 2018, the former motel was still in the Weiland family but was listed for sale.

Two water towers labeled "Bourbon" rise over a town named after booze. When George Turner put a barrel of bourbon out on the porch of his general store to sell to the Irish and Scottish workers building the railroad, the place became known as the Bourbon Store. The main building of the old Bourbon Lodge still stands on the old route.

The Circle Inn got its name because drive-up window patrons had to circle around back. Opened in 1956 just before Bourbon was bypassed, it was sold to Estel (Bud) and Rosella Ware that same year. They sold to their son Bob Ware in 1973. Justin and Josh Ware took over after Bob died in 2011, and the building has been remodeled.

The Missouri Highway Patrol is keeping an eye on traffic for this Missouri Highway Department striping crew at Leasburg in 1948. Leasburg marks the turnoff to Onondaga Cave. The Junction Inn is on the left. It made headlines for a tragic tale of unrequited love in September 1941. A 16-year-old girl who worked there took poison after she failed to win the affections of a boy from Sullivan. (Missouri State Archives.)

Onondaga Cave was once divided in two. George Mook promoted the cave under his land as Missouri Caverns, the first electrically lighted cave in the state. Bob Bradford operated Onondaga, where tourists entered by boat. Missouri Caverns was closer to Route 66, so Mook did all he could to divert traffic to his cave. Lester Dill eventually took over both properties. Onondaga became a state park in 1982.

The Wagon Wheel Motel in Cuba has been in continuous operation since 1934. It was built for Robert and Margaret Martin with stonework by Leo Friesenhan. Other owners included John and Winifred Mathis and William and Sadie Mae Pratt. Pauline and Wayne Roberts took over in 1963. Wayne died in 1980, and Pauline married Harold Armstrong in 1988. With caretaker Roy Mudd, they kept the Wagon Wheel going.

The gas station and café at the Wagon Wheel are shown here with Clyde Mathis at the pumps. The motel began to decline after Pauline Armstrong died in 2003, and its future was in doubt after Harold Armstrong died in 2008. In 2009, Connie Caspers Echols acquired the Wagon Wheel and began a restoration that preserved the charm while adding modern amenities. The former café is now a unique gift shop. (Riva Echols.)

Cuba was laid out in 1857 ahead of construction on the southwest branch of the Pacific Railroad. Wesley Smith suggested the name as a show of support for citizens of Cuba fighting tyrannical Spanish rule. This view looks east toward the Wagon Wheel Motel, with Cuba Drug on the right. The drugstore building now houses the East Office Lounge. The Shell station at right became Spirals Art Gallery.

During the height of the Cold War, in February 1960, Walter Dorf placed this sign at the west entrance to town on Highway 66. The People's Bank of Cuba attracted some notoriety in 1974 with a billboard east of town on Interstate 44 that read "Let us hijack your business to Cuba." Cuba is now known as "Mural City USA" for its numerous historic murals.

A beloved Cuba landmark was lost with the demolition of the Midway Café at Route 66 and Missouri 19 in 2013. Allyne Earls purchased the Midway in 1934 and added a second story with 24 hotel rooms in 1944. When Allyne sold in 1972, the new owner found there were no keys to the restaurant—the doors had never been locked. The Midway was also owned for several years by St. Louis Blues hockey star Noel Picard.

The vintage cottage-style Phillips 66 station across the road was saved from meeting the same fate as the Midway. Paul T. Carr opened this station in 1932. After a series of owners and brands, it was bought by Bill and Lyn Wallis, who founded the Wallis Oil chain of Mobil stations. After Bill died, Lynn began restoring the building in his honor. Joanie Weir opened the Fourway Restaurant here in April 2016.

They really know how to rock in the small community of Fanning. From 2008 to 2015, the 42-foot-tall rocking chair outside of Dan and Carolyn Sanazaro's Fanning Outpost was the largest in the world. It is now known as the Route 66 Rocker. The chair did rock at first but was a terrifying sight as tons of metal swayed back and forth. It was welded down securely to ensure no one was crushed.

Rosati was once known as Knobview. In 1931, the "Little Italy of the Ozarks" was renamed for Joseph Rosati, first bishop of St. Louis. The original settlers were lured from Italy to work at a cotton plantation in Arkansas. They arrived here in 1898 and planted Concord grapes when Italian grapes would not grow. Over 35 grape stands like the Marchi family's, shown here, once lined a four-mile stretch of Highway 66. (Rosati-mo.com.)

Six

HILLS AND STREAMS
PHELPS AND PULASKI COUNTIES

In August 1929, the first section of divided highway on Route 66 was constructed in St. James. Landowner John Pace required the state to construct four blocks of Pace Boulevard (now West James Boulevard) as a condition for granting the right of way. St. James was the home of the first female mayor in Missouri, Mayme Ousley. It is also home to a cool museum devoted entirely to vacuum cleaners. (St. James Library.)

Emory's Garage in St. James was constructed in 1919 on the site of a livery stable erected by Albin H. Emory in 1882. From left to right are James White, Jack Ten Eyck, and Harry Emory Sr. White worked at Emory Garage during his high school years and then went on to open his own garage in St. James. In 2015, his son Jim was elected mayor of the city. (St. James Library.)

When his Mule Trading Post in Pacific was bypassed, Frank Ebling moved to the new route east of Rolla and opened a new place in October 1958. The Mule was later owned by Herb and Jody Baden, then by Jack and Janiece Wittman. Carl and Zelma Smith took over in 2007, and rescued the two-story sign from the old Hillbilly Store on Interstate 44. New ownership renovated the Mule in 2018.

In 1857, George Coppedge wanted to name the seat of the newly created Phelps County for his North Carolina home, Raleigh. Local legend says he pronounced it "Rolla." Rolla is the home of the Missouri University of Science and Technology with its half-sized replica of Stonehenge. Some drivers required a little explanation at the interchanges when the four-lane bypass shown here opened in October 1954. (Missouri State Archives.)

Pierce Petroleum started a chain of first-class hotels for the automobile age and pioneered the use of billboards and free road maps. The Pennant Hotel at Rolla was the second, opening on November 4, 1929. Rowe Carney and his son built the Carney Manor Inn just down the hill in 1956. But it lost access when Interstate 44 opened, and the remodeled Pennant became the Carney Manor Motel in 1963. The Peartree Inn stands here today.

The Pierce Pennant Tavern opened in August 1929 and was operated by Diehl Montgomery. Robert and Margaret Martin operated it as Pennant Café and Motel Martin after selling the Wagon Wheel Hotel in Cuba in 1946. After a 1953 fire, part of the remaining structure was incorporated into a new Motel Martin, which no longer stands. The open area in the foreground is where Interstate 44 runs today.

Richard Schuman started his Tourist City (later Schuman's Motor City) by converting some old chicken coops into cottages. Schuman's complex opened in June 1929 and grew to 40 units, a service station, and a café. The front row of cottages was demolished for the widening of Route 66, and a second story was added to the new units in back. The complex became the Budget Apartments. (Missouri State Archives.)

PINE STREET   ROLLA, MO.   T-21

The Edwin Long Hotel, on the right, was named for former Rolla mayor, banker, and businessman Edwin Long. It opened on March 10, 1931, and just three days later hosted the celebration marking the completion of Route 66 pavement across Missouri. It housed the National Bank of Rolla on the first floor. In 1963, Phelps County Bank moved in. The hotel closed in 1971, and the bank bought the entire building in 1977.

The Totem Pole Trading Post is the oldest active Route 66 business in Missouri. Harry and Edna Cochran opened the trading post topped with a totem pole near Arlington in 1933. There were also six cabins and an early coin-operated laundromat. Ralph and Catherine Jones bought it in 1957 and moved a bit in 1967 when I-44 was constructed. The Totem Pole moved to the west end of Rolla in 1977. (Rich Dinkela.)

Zeno Scheffer and his wife, Loretta, opened Zeno's Studio Motel in 1957 where the new four-lane Route 66 met the City Route at the west end of Rolla. It originally consisted of 20 units. They added the steakhouse in 1959, and the motel eventually grew to 50 rooms. Zeno's remained in the family until closing in 2011 amid increased competition from newer places, and the complex was demolished.

Paul Bennett, known as the "fishing, coon-hunting preacher of the Ozarks," and his wife, Gladys, ran Bennett's Catfish at the Newburg turnoff. Paul's tabernacle was in the back. He drew huge crowds to his revivals and stood trial for slander after accusing a Newburg High School teacher of smoking, drinking, and cursing. Paul died in 1951, and Gladys moved to the new four-lane 66. Bennett's closed during construction of Interstate 44 in 1966.

Monroe Ramsey's place was midway between Rolla and Newburg, so he called it the Centerville Garage. Locals began calling the area Centerville too. But Centerville has disappeared from the map. When the town was incorporated in 1943, it was named for Jimmy Doolittle, leader of the first US bombing raid on Tokyo. Doolittle came to town for the dedication on October 11, 1946. (Steve Rider Collection.)

Road builders have been trying to tame the grade at Arlington since the 1920s. A tangle of alignments starts at Exit 176, Sugar Tree Road. Vernelle's Motel was originally the Gasser Tourist Court, opened in 1938 by E.P. Gasser. Nye Goodridge bought it in 1960. The complex is shown here in 1966 when the liquor store and station were to be torn down for construction of the Interstate 44 service road. The motel at far left remained open and Ed Goodridge followed in his father's footsteps. But a 2005 realignment of I-44 left Vernelle's invisible from the interstate. The motel closed in 2016. (Missouri Department of Transportation.)

John's Modern Cabins, east of Arlington, were originally the Bill and Bess Place, a dance hall and three log cabins operated by Bill and Beatrice "Bessie" Bayless. The dance hall was the scene of a murder on Halloween night in 1935. John Dausch took over in 1951 and became known as "Sunday John" for illegally selling booze on Sunday. He added three frame cabins from Schuman's Tourist City in Rolla. The cabins began slowly returning to nature after he died in 1971, and only one remains. (Missouri Department of Transportation.)

Arlington is tucked below the Interstate 44 bridge, accessible only by a dead-end service road. At the confluence of the Gasconade and Little Piney Rivers, the old resort town has been part of St. Louis, Gasconade, Crawford, Pulaski, and Phelps Counties. Rowe Carney bought the entire village from Fred Pillman for $10,000 in 1946, but his plan to sell it to a film company for a movie set fell through. None of these structures remain. (Steve Rider Collection.)

Original Route 66 at Arlington plunged downhill and turned sharply onto a railroad bridge and a five-span truss built over the Little Piney in 1923. This was the last section of Route 66 in Missouri to be paved. Workers tossed coins into the wet cement to celebrate on January 5, 1931. A new bridge and westbound lanes were built in 1952, and eastbound traffic used the 1931 route until Interstate 44 was completed in 1967. (Missouri State Archives.)

The amazing Stonydell complex, on the west side of the Little Piney, was constructed in 1932 by stonemason George Grant Prewitt and his son Vernon. George Badger did the carpentry work. The swimming pool was 100 feet long and 44 feet wide. Ice-cold water from the Stonydell Spring refreshed the pool through a waterfall. Along the back side of the pool, there were 54 individual changing rooms.

Stonydell straddled both sides of Route 66. The south side also included a restaurant, tavern, service station, and park with playground equipment. There was even a justice of the peace on duty. Beautiful rock cabins were available on the north side of Route 66, along with a picnic area and goldfish pond. Everything on the south side was demolished for the construction of Interstate 44 in 1967. Crumbling ruins remain on the north side. (Steve Rider Collection.)

During the Great Depression, families around Hooker weaved white oak baskets to make a living. The roadside stands of the Wells, Childers, and other families gave the area the nickname "Basketville." William F. Childers is shown with a couple of customers. Basketville began to fade after construction of the four-lane highway. (Elbert I. Childers Collection, Western Historical Manuscript Collection, University of Missouri–Rolla.)

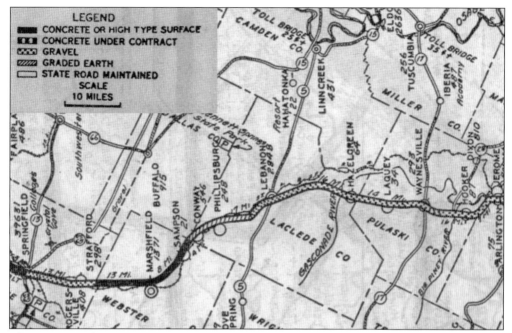

This section of the 1926 Missouri map covers the area between Arlington and Springfield. Route 66 was completely paved only through Webster County at this time. The roadway was mostly gravel, and a dirt section still remained in western Laclede County through Phillipsburg and Conway. But within the next five years, the entire route across the state would be paved.

Traffic west of Rolla quadrupled between 1939 and 1941 due to the construction of Fort Leonard Wood. In the first nine months of 1941, there were 54 deaths and 454 injuries on "Bloody 66" in Phelps, Pulaski, and Laclede Counties. Construction of the four-lane divided route, shown here in December 1941, required blasting through the dolomite at Hooker Hill. The cut was the largest in Missouri at the time. (Missouri State Archives.)

Wartime shortages delayed completion of the entire new four-lane highway in Pulaski County until September 1945. This view looks west from about the same spot as the previous construction photograph. In 1981, this roadway became the last section of Route 66 in Missouri to be bypassed. It is now County Route Z. At the bottom of the hill past the cut, the original alignment leads into Devils Elbow. (Missouri State Archives.)

The Elbow Inn was originally the Munger-Moss sandwich shop, opened by Howard Moss after he married Nellie Munger in 1936. Jessie and Pete Hudson later took over, but they moved to Lebanon when the bypass opened. The Elbow Inn became known for the assortment of patrons' brassieres hanging from the ceiling. The inn was flooded in 2017, but owners Terry and Susie Robertson restored it with help from a host of volunteers.

Devils Elbow took its name from a sharp bend in the river that frustrated railroad tie hackers as they floated tie rafts down the Big Piney. The bridge at Devils Elbow is a two-span riveted Parker through truss built in 1923 and renovated in 2014. In 1930, Dwight Rench constructed the distinctive Devils Elbow Café at right, operated in conjunction with his Cedar Lodge. The café burned in 1970.

Dorothy McCoy's father, Charles, ran McCoy's store and hotel, which also briefly housed a dance hall. Dorothy married Jiggs Miller, and they opened Miller's Market next door, which became Allman's and then Shelden's Market. The flood of 2017 destroyed the remnants of McCoy's and swamped the market just weeks after the Devils Elbow Historic District was listed in the National Register of Historic Places. (Terry Primas.)

The original alignment through Devils Elbow (now Teardrop Road) was never paved in concrete, because a dam and reservoir proposed at Arlington in 1929 would have inundated the village and the road. The pavement changes from asphalt to concrete above the projected water level, where this wall and overlook were constructed. The top of the wall offers a scenic view of the railroad bridge, the river, and the valley below.

The 1945 bridge that carried four-lane Highway 66 over the Big Piney River is shown here under construction. It includes three spandrel arches and five arched girder approach spans, all supported by concrete spill-through open piers. The bridge is still in use today. The Piney Cabins, off Tank Road at the west end of the bridge, are a fine example of the "giraffe rock" exteriors so prevalent in the Ozarks. (Missouri State Archives.)

Morgan Heights consisted of a hotel, a café, cabins, and a gas station where Route 66 originally met Missouri 28. This view looks east, with Missouri 28 splitting off to the left toward Dixon and Missouri 14 (later US 66) continuing down the hill toward Devils Elbow. This section was cut off by construction of the four-lane highway in the 1940s. The old two-lane "ghost highway" is a great place to explore today. (Missouri State Archives.)

Pulaski County changed forever in 1940, when the US Army broke ground for Fort Leonard Wood and 32,000 workers descended on the area. Businesses offering all kinds of entertainment sprang up practically overnight at the wye where Route 66 intersected with Missouri 17 leading to the fort. Several dance halls, including one in a 60-by-120-foot tent, offered alcohol and "dime-a-dance girls."

In just six months, over 1,500 new buildings were constructed at Fort Leonard Wood. More than 300,000 soldiers trained here during World War II. The base was deactivated in 1946 but reactivated during the Korean War. Today, Fort Leonard Wood is home to the Army's Maneuver Support Center, where more than 80,000 initial entry and engineer, chemical defense, and military police enlisted soldiers are trained each year.

Waynesville was established in 1834 and named after Revolutionary War hero Gen. "Mad Anthony" Wayne. Roubidoux Spring, in present-day Laughlin Park, was a camping site on the Cherokee Trail of Tears. Highway 66 into town was paved in 1930, and the village remained quiet until the construction of Fort Leonard Wood. Then the population boomed from about 400 to 3,000 within a few weeks.

William Walton McDonald built the Waynesville House on the stagecoach route between St. Louis and Springfield about 1860. It was originally two connected log cabins, and a second story was added in the 1880s. It was known as the Tourist Inn during the Route 66 era but closed in the early 1960s. A foundation was formed to save the Old Stagecoach Stop after it was condemned in 1982, and it is now a museum. (Old Stagecoach Stop.)

The Confederate flag flew over the Pulaski County Courthouse from April 1861 until federal forces arrived in June 1862. A new courthouse was constructed in 1873 but burned in 1902. Henry Hohenschild designed the courthouse that opened in 1903 and was the seat of government in Pulaski County until 1989. It is now the home of the Pulaski County Courthouse Museum, filled with exhibits on area history.

Loren Claude Rigsby and his wife, Evielena, opened their service station across from the Pulaski County Courthouse in 1924, when the roadway out front was still Missouri 14. They operated the station for 33 years. Their home next door became Nona's Kitchen Restaurant. It was originally a log cabin built in the 1870s for Judge V.B. Hill's family. The station building also still stands.

A bridge of five 80-foot concrete-filled spandrel arches was constructed over Roubidoux Creek at Waynesville in 1923. Prior to that time, the old road turned to run around the square behind the courthouse to the bridge at North Street. The piers of the old steel bridge are still visible. The concrete bridge was widened on the north side in 1939 and still carries traffic as of 2018, although a new span is in the planning stages.

Robert A. Bell was mayor of Waynesville during the critical time when Fort Leonard Wood was constructed, and he later became a judge. From 1925 until 1937, he operated the Bell Hotel and the café, cabins, and garage next door. The hotel was later operated by Mr. and Mrs. W.L. Thomas, who kept the Bell name. Extensively remodeled, the former hotel is now the Waynesville Memorial Chapel Funeral Home.

"OUT OF THE SMOKE ZONE-INTO THE OZONE"

PIPPIN PLACE ON THE GASCONADE WAYNESVILLE MO

There were over two dozen resorts in the Gasconade River valley, including Gascozark Hills, the Eden, Lew Walker's Resort, and Pippin Place west of Waynesville. Pippin Place was the most elaborate, established by Dr. Bland Pippin. The clubhouse was completed in 1914. Guests included Joan Crawford and Douglas Fairbanks Jr. The resort ceased operation in 1964, and the clubhouse burned in June 1984. Only ruins remain.

In September 1952, crews are blasting along Roubidoux Creek to construct the new route bypassing Waynesville. Completion of the 19-mile section of divided highway was announced on January 1, 1956. The last US 66 project awarded in Missouri prior to the Interstate Highway Act of 1956 was a 9.1-mile relocation between Buckhorn and the Laclede County line approved in late 1955. It was completed in November 1957. (Missouri State Archives.)

The scene of this accident is the D&D Market and Café at Buckhorn, owned and operated by brothers Elmer and Don Deutschman from 1948 until 1972. It was just west of where the Interstate Food Market is today. Buckhorn was named for a tavern on the stagecoach line that had a pair of deer antlers hanging above the door. The community was annexed by Waynesville in 2003.

The Normandy hotel, restaurant, and gas station was established in 1932 and became a pretty rowdy roadhouse. After it closed in the 1970s, the local volunteer fire department used it for practice and burned it down. The entrance pillars that stand on the south side of Route 66 near the turnoff for the Pulaski County–Fort Leonard Wood Shrine Club are the only remnants. The remainder of the site is now a quarry.

From 1926 until 1930, Route 66 passed through Laquey (prounounced "lake-way"), named after Joseph Laquey, who established the post office in 1899. The original route used present-day Routes P, AA, and AB. The new paved highway followed today's Missouri 17. The A&E Station, cabins, and grocery operated by R.E. Riggs was close to the three-way stop where the original and post-1930 alignments meet. The building has been altered and covered in aluminum siding. It is deteriorated but still stands.

Frank A. Jones combined the words "Gasconade" and "Ozark" into "Gascozark" for his business on Highway 66. He also built the Gascozark Hills Resort. The Gascozark Café later became the Spinning Wheel. It sat abandoned and was overgrown with vegetation until a local car club and the Boy Scouts cleaned up the lot in 2016. Across the highway is the Gascozark Trading Post, originally known as Caldwell's.

Seven

THE HEART OF MISSOURI
LACLEDE AND WEBSTER COUNTIES

The 1923 bridge over the Gasconade River consists of one 80-foot Warren pony truss, two 161-foot Parker through truss spans, and one 123-foot Pratt through truss. After Interstate 44 was completed, Old 66 became the service road. The bridge was closed due to safety concerns in December 2014. The Missouri Department of Transportation began construction of a new span in 2018. The old bridge was allowed to stand while preservation efforts continued. (Steve Rider Collection.)

The new roadway creating four-lane Route 66 was under construction at the Gasconade River when this photograph looking east was taken in March 1959. Note the temporary connector roads. St. Louis businessman Stanley M. Riggs built the Eden Resort, on the right, in the 1920s. Walter and Helen Dickinson bought the Eden in 1946 and ran it until the early 1970s. Nothing remains of the resort today. (Missouri State Archives.)

Lebanon was originally named Wyota for an Indian village. Jessie and Pete Hudson owned the Munger-Moss sandwich shop at Devils Elbow when it was bypassed. They bought the Chicken Shanty Restaurant at Lebanon in 1946 and added the Munger Moss Motel next door. The original seven cottages had rooms at each end and garages in the middle. They were later connected, and the complex grew to 71 rooms. (Ramona Lehman.)

The neon sign at the Munger Moss still serves as a beacon for Route 66 travelers. Pete Hudson, the owner at the time, was inspired by the dramatic sign at the Rest Haven in Springfield and added the marquee with the sweeping arrow in 1955. Bob and Ramona Lehman have operated this treasure since moving from Iowa in 1971. The sign was restored in 2010 with assistance from the Route 66 Association of Missouri and the National Park Service.

On June 10, 1950, Glenn Wrinkle opened Wrink's Food Market on Route 66 on the east end of Lebanon. He operated the market until February 21, 2005, and died in March 2005 at the age of 82. One of Glenn's sons, Terry Wrinkle, reopened the store in 2007, but it closed again in 2009. It then briefly housed another business that also closed. Glenn's granddaughter Katie Hapner brought Wrink's back to life in June 2017.

Newlyweds Lois and Emis Spears spent their honeymoon with his parents counting cars along the roadside in search of a good location for a tourist camp. In 1927, they settled in on the gravel Route 66 at Lebanon and called their place Camp Joy. The sign at the exit read, "Teach Your Baby to Say Camp Joy." Later known as the Joy Motel, it remained in the family until 1971 and closed in the 1980s. Only a single cabin remains today.

Andy Liebl's Street Car Grill occupied two old streetcars salvaged from Springfield, Missouri. The diner was known for "Andy's Famous Fried Domestic Rabbit." It also advertised "The Finest Food in the Ozarks" and "Lebanon's Cleanest Café." The Street Car Grill closed in 1961. It was located just east of Carter and Lawson's gas station, which became Orchard Hills Liquor.

Honorary colonel Arthur T. Nelson donated the right-of-way through his apple orchard for Missouri 14 (later US 66). Nelson's Tavern, at Highway 66 and Missouri 5, opened on January 21, 1930. It never actually sold alcohol and was later known as Nelson's Hotel. Lush gardens surrounded the hotel, and the interior was filled with plants (including palm trees) and exotic caged birds. "Nelsonville" was leveled for a supermarket in 1958. (Lebanon–Laclede County Library.)

While working on the Missouri displays at the 1933 Century of Progress Exposition in Chicago, Arthur Nelson saw a fountain with colored lights synchronized with music. Nelson said his design for a tourist court came to him later in a dream. Across 66 from the Nelson Hotel, records played over a loudspeaker at the lighted fountain in the Dream Village. The entire complex was demolished in 1977. (Lebanon–Laclede County Library.)

The first contract signed under the Interstate Highway Act on August 2, 1956, was for 13.8 miles of four-lane highway between Lebanon and Hazelgreen. A new section, opened in December 1957 at Phillipsburg, bypassed this Frisco Railroad underpass with a clearance of just 13 feet, 5 inches. Some truckers had to let air out of their tires to get through. The old underpass remains on present-day Route W. (Missouri State Archives.)

Conway Court Highway 66 Conway Mo

S.W. "Sim" Harris had the market cornered at the intersection with Route J in Conway. His two gas stations and Harris Modern Camp occupied three corners, and the family home was on the fourth. His son Barney opened the Harris Café next to one of the stations in 1931 and later moved to the four-lane route. Old Route 66, now Route CC, is a nice drive well away from the interstate between Conway and Marshfield.

In 1940, a prominent attorney built the Abbylee Court and Café "Among the Trees" west of Conway. Some of the cabins were used regularly by a group of bootleggers. Ernest Cunningham, a mail carrier from Kansas, took over in 1949, and the café burned in 1950. By 1963, the Abbylee was no longer a motel. The seven white clapboard cabins were converted to monthly rentals and still stand, along with the old sign.

Off Interstate 44 at Exit 107, a nondescript ruin is crumbling among the choking weeds. It was once one of the most memorable places on Highway 66. Kermit and Letha Lowery wanted to make sure travelers would remember the name of the café they opened in 1952, so they called it the Garbage Can. Known for its little round pies, a recipe Letha inherited from the Harris Café in Conway, the Garbage Can closed in 1973. (Missy Lowery.)

The Skyline was the café at the original Marshfield Airport and golf course. Herman and Cleta Pearce built it in 1947 on the site of the old Trask's Place Station and Café. Except for the propeller on the wall, the interior was typical of the small cafés in the Ozarks. The Skyline was expanded in 1957 using a building moved from Evangel College, and the country club purchased the site after the café closed in May 1963.

Route 66 in Marshfield is named in honor of local Edwin Hubble, the astronomer who proved the existence of galaxies outside the Milky Way. A replica of the Hubble Space Telescope sits on the courthouse lawn. The Sinclair Tourist Camp at the west entrance to town was operated by Marshall Lane, who built a new station with his son-in-law after World War II. It later became the R and J Café. A gas station still stands here today.

When the new four-lane US 66 was constructed, Spur Drive was built to connect with Marshfield. The intersection shown here in June 1955 became one of the deadliest on Route 66 due to the high speeds and cross traffic. Prior to 1957, "reasonable and prudent" was the only speed limit on Missouri highways. On the left is the Spur Café, which was owned and operated by George and Jean Barnes.

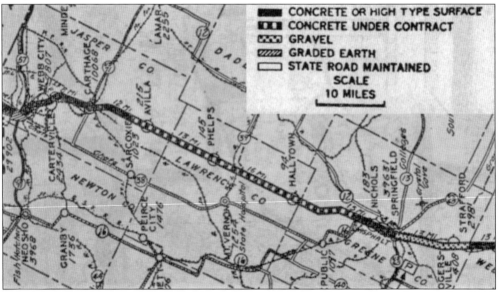

From Springfield to the west, Route 66 was either paved or under contract to be paved in 1926. The first section of concrete highway in Missouri was the 7.4-mile section from Webb City to the Kansas state line, poured in 1920 and designated Federal Aid Project No. 2. Construction was overseen by John Malang of the Joplin Special Road District, who later became state superintendent of highways.

Eight

BIRTHPLACE OF 66
GREENE AND LAWRENCE COUNTIES

Strafford had to do an about-face when Route 66 came through its backyard in June 1928. The new road followed an old alley between the Frisco station and the main street, forcing business owners to build new entrances. Douglas Potter's Garage, at right, became a machine shop in 1969 and is now the Route 66 Pup Stop. As of 2018, the town was planning a historical park next to city hall with replicas of early landmarks. (Missouri State Archives.)

Route 66 entered Springfield on Division Street until Kearney Street was extended east in 1928. The historic route then followed Glenstone Avenue to St. Louis Street and exited the square on College Street. This sign was on the bypass route established in 1938 that followed Kearney Street to the West Bypass (US 160). During the 1960s, City Route 66 turned off Glenstone Avenue to Chestnut Street (Missouri 266) to rejoin the historic route at College Street. (Missouri State Archives.)

Hillary Brightwell took over Richard Chapman's gas station on Kearney Street in October 1936. He and his wife, Mary, began adding motel units in 1947 and ran the Rest Haven until 1979. The current sign was erected in 1953 and made by Springfield Neon. It inspired Pete Hudson, owner of the Munger Moss in Lebanon, to erect a similar sign for his motel. As of 2018, the Rest Haven is deteriorated but still in business.

On the southwest corner of Glenstone Avenue and Kearney Street, the Rock Village combined the native rock veneer of the Ozarks with glass accents and deco styling. In addition to cabins, there were rooms in the main building. The complex changed hands repeatedly and was remodeled several times before being demolished for the Solar Inn. An America's Best Value Inn is located here today. (Missouri State Archives.)

Virgil Al "Big Boy" Murphy opened Big Boy's Auto Court in 1938, and the gas station out front was housed in an old Springfield Traction Company trolley car. A sign out front read, "Hi there: Stop. We've been looking for you today." Big Boy's became the Sands Motel in 1959. The Sands was demolished in 1972 for a supermarket, and the site at 1828 North Glenstone Avenue is now a Brown Derby liquor store.

The Lily-Tulip Corporation chose Springfield as the site of its new plant on December 6, 1951. The plant, with a giant cup-shaped entrance, employed up to 1,200 people. Sold to Owens-Illinois in 1968, it was taken over by a newly formed Lily-Tulip in 1981 and became Sweetheart Cup in 1989. Solo acquired the plant in 2004 and closed it down in 2011. The building was converted to warehouse space, and the cup was removed. (Missouri State Archives.)

A new viaduct carrying Glenstone Avenue over the Frisco Railroad tracks opened in 1939. This view looks south, with the Rittenhouse Market, later Glenstone Market, on the left. Across St. Louis Street is the White Rose gas station, which became a Standard station operated by Voytil "Sandy" Sanders. Rex Wilson's Standard is on the right, past the Tydol station. It was relocated in 1954 for construction of the new Rail Haven Motel office. (Missouri State Archives.)

Brothers Lawrence and Elwyn Lippman opened the eight Rail Haven Cottages in 1938 at Glenstone and St. Louis Streets and advertised "Look for the Rail Fence." The cabins were connected in 1940, and it became the Rail Haven Motel following an expansion and construction of a new office in 1954. In 1994, Gordon Elliott bought the fading motel and turned it into a nostalgic but modern gem, the Route 66 Rail Haven. (Rail Haven Motel.)

GRAHAM'S MODERN TOURIST COURT

During the Jim Crow era, James and Zelma Graham welcomed everyone at their tourist court. The cabins were behind their Graham's Rib Station at the present-day Chestnut Expressway and Washington Avenue. Little Richard, Ella Fitzgerald, Pearl Bailey, and other entertainers stayed there when performing at the Shrine Mosque. Entrepreneur Alberta Ellis also served African Americans at her hotel on Benton Street.

The Kentwood Arms Hotel,
Springfield, Missouri

John T. Woodruff saw the need for lodging serving travelers on the new highway and built the Kentwood Arms Hotel on St. Louis Street in 1926. Acquired by Southwest Missouri State University in 1984, it is now the Kentwood Hall dormitory. Woodruff also built his landmark office building, the Colonial Hotel, and the Sansone Hotel. In addition, he served as the first president of the US 66 Highway Association.

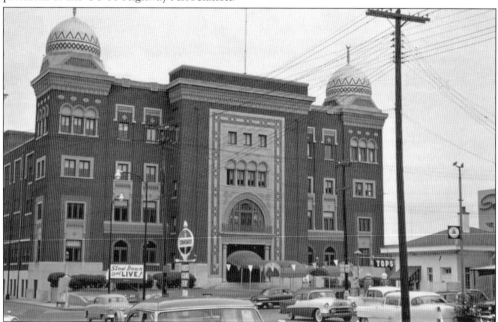

The Moorish-style Shrine Mosque was dedicated on November 3, 1923. It was built as the home of the Abou Ben Adhem Temple Shriners but hosted many civic events. Harry S. Truman was an honorary member. Other notables who appeared there include John F. Kennedy, Richard Nixon, Gen. John J. Pershing, Will Rogers, and Elvis Presley. The building was renovated in 1987, and the auditorium now seats 4,750. (Richard Crabtree.)

Springfield was terrorized for two months in 1953 as deadly hooded cobras slithered around. Exotic pet store owner Reo Mowrer denied they were his, while police played snake charmer music through a loudspeaker hoping to lure them out, apparently not knowing that cobras are deaf. Eleven were eventually dispatched, and Mowrer left town. Years later, a man admitted that he had released the snakes as a youth because a fish he bought from Mowrer died.

The Gillioz Theater opened on October 11, 1926. Road builder and theater operator M.E. Gillioz could not find a location on the proposed Highway 66, so he built a block to the north, leased a 20-foot-wide frontage on St. Louis Street for the entrance, and linked it to the theater 130 feet away. The 1,100-seat "Glorious Gillioz," where Elvis Presley watched a movie before his 1956 concert, closed in 1980 but was restored in 2006.

The first of the Pierce Pennant terminals opened on July 16, 1928, on St. Louis Street at Kimbrough Avenue. It consisted of three buildings, including a bus terminal and a car wash. The restaurant was operated by the former manager of the Harvey House at the Frisco station. The Greyhound terminal moved in 1974, and this building was demolished in 1979 for the Discovery Center parking lot.

A historical marker on the public square in Springfield marks the approximate spot where James "Wild Bill" Hickock killed Dave Tutt in a duel over a gambling debt. In 1911, the city built a roundabout for the trolley system in the center of the square. It became known as "the Pie" and was removed in 1947 to allow cross traffic. The Heer's Department Store building at left is now luxury lofts. (Missouri State Archives.)

After the Pie in the public square was removed in 1947, the corners were used for parking, as seen in this 1953 view. The parking was removed, and the middle of the square became a landscaped plaza designed by Lawrence Halprin in 1970. Several businesses were killed off when the square was closed to vehicle traffic in 1973, but the streets were reopened in 1984, and a major renovation took place in 2011. (Missouri State Archives.)

Steam blew from the nostrils of this slobbering long-necked beast, a familiar sight on US 66. "Snortin' Norton" was the mascot of Campbell 66 Express trucking, founded in Springfield by Frank Campbell, shown here. The company grew to serve 22 states before it was bankrupted by deregulation and looting from within. A fleet of Snortin' Norton trailers can be seen today at Rich Henry's Rabbit Ranch in Staunton, Illinois.

The Conoco station operated by Paul Wilcox had a historical marker built into it. It reads: "Site of the first school in what is now Springfield, built by pioneers, 1832, of small logs with mud and stick chimney, loose plank floor, and three legged benches. Joseph Rountree first teacher." The marker was salvaged when the building was demolished in 1984 and now stands on the site, a parking lot at 601 College Street.

The Trail's End Motor Court, on the bypass route, opened in 1948 and featured a neon sign with a Native American on horseback. The sign has been altered, and the complex is now the Rancho Apartments at East Kearney Street and Delaware Avenue. The Rock Fountain Court, now the Melinda Apartments at 2400 West College Street, is another surviving example of the typical Ozark motor court finished in rock veneer.

When Sheldon "Red" Cheney rigged an intercom at Red's Giant Hamburg (the "-er" would not fit on the sign), he may have created the first restaurant drive-through. Red and his wife, Julia, also ran the 66 Motel here from 1948 until 1955. Red's closed on December 14, 1984, and was demolished in 1997. A replica of the sign stands at the Birthplace of Route 66 Roadside Park on West College Street. (Southwest Missouri State University.)

Sandra Lyle of Springfield, Miss Missouri 1962, took part in the dedication ceremonies for the first section of Interstate 44 bypassing the city. The new section ran eight miles between Glenstone Avenue and Hazeltine Road and was dedicated on October 5. Its completion provided drivers with a continuous four-lane highway from the Meramec River west of St. Louis to past Springfield. (Missouri State Archives.)

Neon beckons at R&S Memorial Decorations west of Springfield, where John Schweke and his wife, Alexa, transformed a crumbling ruin into a Route 66 success story. They preserved the original Graystone Heights Modern Cabins, opened in 1935 by Ben and Margaret Brewer. The property was purchased by Russell and Betty Schweke and became R&S Floral in 1963. The sign was restored in 2014.

The sturdy limestone walls of this abandoned structure stand in the ghost town of Plano. Often mistakenly listed as a casket factory, it was actually a general store constructed in 1902 and operated by the Jackson family. A meeting and dance hall on the second floor was also used as a church. The family did run a mortuary and undertaker's parlor with caskets for sale across the county road.

Antique collectors used to come to Halltown from miles around. In the 1950s, there were at least seven antique stores in the town of fewer than 100 people. Jerry and Thelma White operated the Halltown Mercantile. Thelma passed away in April 2010, and Jerry closed the store following the holidays in 2016. Halltown is now a tranquil place on the "Ghost Stretch" of Old 66 known for its abundance of roadside ruins.

Fred Mason's garage, café, and cabins at Paris Springs was named Gay Parita after his wife. Gay died in 1953, and the station burned in 1955. Gary and Fred Turner built this replica of Gay Parita on the site in 2007. It became a Route 66 icon where Gary made "friends for life." The Route 66 community lost Gary on January 22, 2015, but his daughter Barbara Turner Barnes and her husband, George, carry on his legacy. (Turner family.)

The "town" of Spencer consisted of a café, barbershop, service station, and garage owned by Sidney Casey. It was bypassed in 1961. In 2008, Francis and Mary Lynn Ryan bought the property from Sidney Casey's grandson and began restoring the row of structures.

Old Route 66, now Missouri 96, continues straight as an arrow west through the fading remnants of Heatonville, Albatross, Phelps, Rescue, and Plew. Bill Tiller's station at Phelps stood crumbling beside the roadway for 40 years after the community was bypassed. (John Margolies Roadside America Archives, Library of Congress.)

Nine

ON TO KANSAS
JASPER COUNTY

Outlaws Bonnie Parker and Clyde Barrow were staying at the Log City Camp at Avilla in the early 1930s while a highway patrol troop meeting also took place, but they laid low, and the officers never knew. Carl Stansbury built the camp in 1926, and Billy Baker owned it for years. Log City included 18 cottages and cabins as well as a tavern and dining room across from the rival Forest Park Camp. The site became an auto body shop.

Highway 66 originally angled into Carthage from the east to Central Avenue, while US 71 entered on North Garrison Avenue. Alternate 66 was created when the "New Mile," shown here, was dedicated in June 1930. It used present-day Route V to North Garrison Avenue, turning south to meet the mainline at Central Avenue. The main route was realigned in 1954 to follow present-day Missouri 96, and the Alternate 66 designation was removed.

The Jasper County Courthouse, on the Carthage town square, is made of Carthage stone, which was also used for Missouri's state capitol. The courthouse was dedicated on October 9, 1895. Architect Maximilian Orlop also designed several other elaborate courthouses, notably in Dallas and New Orleans. City leaders in Joplin and Carthage actually came to blows over the site of the county seat, so a courthouse was also built in Joplin as a compromise. The Joplin courthouse burned in 1911.

Arthur and Ilda Boots opened the Boots Court in 1939 and advertised "A Radio in Every Room." It was operated by Reuben and Rachel Asplin for many years, and Clark Gable is said to have stayed there. It was nearly demolished before sisters Debye Harvey and Priscilla Bledsaw began restoration in 2011. The Boots is now the most authentic vintage Route 66 motel in Missouri, complete with a radio in every room.

Arthur and Ilda Boots divorced in 1941. Arthur and his son Robert moved across the street from the motel and opened the streamline Boots Drive-In in 1946. From 1947 until 1957, radio station KDMO broadcast *Breakfast from the Crossroads of America* live from the restaurant. The Boots Drive-In closed in 1970, but the building is still recognizable today. It currently houses the Great Plains Credit Union.

There were once six drive-in theaters with "66" in the name, but only one survives, the 66 Drive-In west of Carthage. V.F. Naramore and W.D. Bradfield opened it on September 22, 1949, with a showing of *Two Guys from Texas*. The 66 Drive-In closed in 1985 and was an auto salvage yard until Mark and Dixie Goodman began restoration. The drive-in reopened on April 18, 1998. Nathan and Amy McDonald bought it in 2017.

Jasper County is part of the Tri-State lead mining district, and towns such as Carterville boomed until the mines began shutting down after World War II. Jackson Bulger and his brother Judd starting selling cars on Route 66 in 1946, and the Bulger Motor Company is a great stop for photographs today with its old cars out front. Larry Tamminen's Super-TAM, an ice cream parlor filled with thousands of Superman collectibles, is also in Carterville.

Route 66 curves into Webb City past the brick buildings of the Webb Corporation, in the same location since 1881 making metal equipment for fabricators. Tradition says that John C. Webb laid out the town after finding lead on his property. A large area that was once the desolate site of the Sucker Flats Mine is now beautiful King Jack Park. "Jack" is slang for zinc ore. The park includes the 32-foot-tall *Praying Hands* sculpture.

Original 66 in Joplin jogged through Royal Heights over Zora Street, Florida Avenue, and Utica and Euclid Streets. It was relocated occasionally due to collapsing mine shafts, and Euclid Street follows the old route of the interurban electric railway that linked towns in three states. The Shamrock Inn and Phillips 66 station at 2312 Utica Street opened in the 1920s. The station closed in 1959, and Dale Holly ran a barbershop here from 1962 until 2012.

The 1937–1945 alignment, later Alternate 66, came down Main Street in Joplin to turn west on Seventh Street toward the Kansas state line. The final alignment used Range Line Road to Seventh Street. This September 1949 view captures construction of the Seventh Street Viaduct over the Missouri Pacific Railroad west of Range Line Road. (Missouri State Archives.)

Prior to the Route 66 era, most travel was by rail, and the great hotels in Joplin were located on Main Street downtown. The Keystone Hotel was named after Pennsylvania, the "Keystone State" and home state of owner E.Z. Wallower. The six-story structure opened in 1892. The Keystone dominated the skyline until it was demolished in 1968 during the urban renewal craze that wiped out 40 acres of structures downtown.

HOTEL CONNOR — JOPLIN, MO. 5A-H559

Millionaire Thomas Connor had torn down his old Joplin Hotel and a new one was under construction when he died in 1907. The new hotel was named in his honor. Once the finest in Joplin, the Hotel Connor was being prepared for demolition in 1978 when the weakened walls suddenly collapsed. Two workers died, and one was trapped for 82 hours. The Joplin City Library stands on the site today.

LITTLE KING'S COURT, 2207 W. 7TH ST., (U. S. 66) JOPLIN, MO.

Two of the largest tourist camps in Joplin were Dick Cole and Harry M. Bennett's Koronado Kourts and R.M. Sharp's Little Kings Motor Court, shown here. They each had about 60 units. Interstate 44 opened in 1957, and modern motels clustered on South Range Line Road. They advertised locations on the "US 66 Bypass," although Route 66 never officially went south of Seventh Street.

Wilder's, Inc.
1216 Main Street
Joplin, Missouri
Phone 723

Good Things to Eat and Drink
Choice Steaks
Southern Fried Chicken
Air Conditioned

Wilder's Restaurant is a few blocks south of Route 66 at 1216 South Main Street. Verne Wilder originally operated a pharmacy here beginning in 1930. He added a restaurant called the Southern Buffett by 1933. In 1936, he had converted all of the space to Wilder's Restaurant. Mike and Marsha Pawlus have operated Wilder's since 1996, and the neon sign on the rooftop was restored in 2018.

SCHIFFERDECKER GOLF COURSE AND CLUB HOUSE, JOPLIN, MO.

Electric Park was an amusement park with a roller coaster, rides, sideshows, and a zoo from 1909 to 1912. In 1913, Charles Schifferdecker donated the 40-acre site to the city. Schifferdecker Park now covers 160 acres and includes the Joplin Mineral and History Museums. Joplin citizens and businesses donated the funds to build the Schifferdecker Public Golf Course. It opened on June 29, 1922.

Yankees slugger Mickey Mantle was born in the nearby Route 66 town of Commerce, Oklahoma. He played shortstop for the Joplin Miners in 1950, leading the Western Association with a batting average of .383 and 26 homers. From 1957 to 1965, Mantle was a partner in the Holiday Inn at 2600 Range Line Road. It was open until 1980, and a big-box retailer is located on the site today.

On June 25, 1974, Route 66 was officially decertified between Chicago and the I-44 exit east of Joplin. Joplin then served as the eastern terminus of Route 66 until the remaining 1,162 miles were decertified on June 27, 1985. The last Route 66 signs in Missouri, from the I-44 exit at Scotland to the Kansas state line and on the business loop in Joplin, came down without ceremony on July 24, 1985. (Missouri State Archives.)

DISCOVER THOUSANDS OF LOCAL HISTORY BOOKS FEATURING MILLIONS OF VINTAGE IMAGES

Arcadia Publishing, the leading local history publisher in the United States, is committed to making history accessible and meaningful through publishing books that celebrate and preserve the heritage of America's people and places.

Find more books like this at
www.arcadiapublishing.com

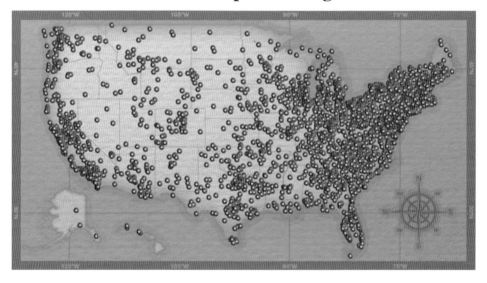

Search for your hometown history, your old stomping grounds, and even your favorite sports team.

Consistent with our mission to preserve history on a local level, this book was printed in South Carolina on American-made paper and manufactured entirely in the United States. Products carrying the accredited Forest Stewardship Council (FSC) label are printed on 100 percent FSC-certified paper.

MADE IN THE